Praise for *Ordinary Blessings for the Christmas Season*

"Filled with ancient truths and modern realities, the seasonal blessings in this book flow from Carlson's sacred gift of noticing. Her honest wonderings and reflective words invite us to exhale, reminding us that we aren't alone–and never have been."

–Kayla Craig, author of *Every Season Sacred: Reflections, Prayers, and Invitations to Nourish Your Soul and Nurture Your Family throughout the Year* and *To Light Their Way: A Collection of Prayers and Liturgies for Parents*; creator of Liturgies for Parents

"Christmas holds vastly different experiences for each person, and yet Meta Herrick Carlson has the gift of naming the complex realities beside the vulnerable wonder. She paints blessing into the ordinary, giving each passing occurrence a voice and community. Through the blessings inspired by many human hearts, Meta reminds us that amid the many layers, the simple is true: 'God becomes flesh because your ordinary is worthy of divine interest, presence, and love.' Giving the ordinary a blessing ritualizes not just the beautiful; it names the true human spectrum and this God who sees it all and continues to dwell with us."

–Rev. Jenny Sung, "Free Range Pastor," and founder and codirector of One Dance Company

"The holiday season poses a mixed bag for many. While balancing different spiritual traditions, many struggle with chaotic family systems, grief, untold joys, and unmet expectations. Is there a resource that can speak to all of these things? I found this book to be so helpful in grounding me, pointing to a possibility of peace both in church and at home. The flow of the poems, meditations, and prayers goes across denominational lines and is a breath of fresh air."

—**Robert Monson**, writer, theologian, and codirector of enfleshed

"You don't have any prayer book like this (yet). Meta Herrick Carlson has a poet's eyes, a pastor's heart, and the grit of a witness to beautiful, complicated holidays with beautiful, complicated humans. At times tender and funny, particular and profound, her poignant words reach into the muddled heart of this season. *Ordinary Blessings for the Christmas Season* holds the full complexity of Christmas. Give yourself the gift of blessings you actually need, trustworthy and true."

—**Laura Kelly Fanucci**, author of
Everyday Sacrament: The Messy Grace of Parenting and *To Bless Our Callings: Prayers, Poems, and Hymns to Celebrate Vocation*

"This book is for anyone yearning to go through the Christmas season with intentionality. We know the season can be overfull; we know we can feel a bit untethered from its richness. Meta Herrick Carlson's words facilitate more space to notice lovely things, be honest in our experiences, and connect with God in the midst of real life this Christmas."

—**Meredith Anne Miller**, pastor and author of *Woven: Nurturing a Faith Your Kid Doesn't Have to Heal From*

"Delightful, refreshing, and oh so true, *Ordinary Blessings for the Christmas Season* is both a perfect stocking stuffer and a church resource for the season. The pressure to fill Christmas with magic and joy can make it too frantic to enjoy. Naming the grief, oddity, expectations, and fatigue of Christmas, Meta Herrick Carlson reminds us we are not alone, and we are deeply loved. She breathes life back into the ordinary and sacred Christmas story, both ancient and modern. These prayers, poems, and blessings embrace us right where we are. God comes near, loving us at family gatherings, church, and fifth-grade concerts, loving us by paying attention, cutting through consumerism to be God-with-us. In these pages is permission to rest, to winter, to claim our freedom, and to look again and see God in every nook and cranny of Christmas."

—**Ellie Roscher**, author of *The Embodied Path* and coauthor of *12 Tiny Things*

"Meta Herrick Carlson sure does know how to be a blessing! Offering everyday blessings for everyday people, *Ordinary Blessings for the Christmas Season* is that circle of light for the season of light. It invokes the power and promise of the Divine. Meta offers us words and images that create awareness, wholeness, and belonging. This gift will offer healing and strength for many Christmas seasons to come."

—**Rev. Babette Chatman**, pastor and director of campus ministry, Augsburg University

"Meta Herrick Carlson has a way of blessing real moments with honesty and care that brings me to tears every time. This is especially true in the complicated soup of feelings around the holiday season. She names the hard and the holy, the peaceful and the painful, the brutal and the beautiful, with care and candor and gorgeous honesty. These blessings are a gift in every season, and so is Meta."

—**Natalia Terfa**, pastor, author of *Uplift*, and host of the *Cafeteria Christian* podcast

"As a fan of *Ordinary Blessings*, I'm delighted there's now the gift of ordinary blessings for Advent and Christmas! These blessings honor the sacred moments of the season alongside the raw emotions that surprise and unnerve us, and they name the complicated beauty of our lives and loves that fills this time of year. Carlson's blessings make more visible God-with-us, Emmanuel, and unearth the holy wisdom found in honoring blessing in each day."

—**Dr. Deanna A. Thompson**, author of
Hoping for More and *Glimpsing Resurrection*;
director of the Lutheran Center for Faith, Values,
and Community; and Martin E. Marty Regents
Chair in Religion and the Academy
at St. Olaf College

"It's the details of these blessings and all of Meta's blessings that strike me—the holy 'noticing' of the small things that are, of course, ultimately everything. She so beautifully puts to words the weight and wonder that exist in this life if only we pause and notice. These blessings are perfect for reflection, to weave into a sermon, or to savor with a morning cup of coffee. *Ordinary Blessings for the Christmas Season* will be a blessing to you!"

—**Rev. Dr. Ruth E. Hetland**, creator and owner of
ConseCrate Subscription Box, LLC

"Meta Herrick Carlson has captured the strata of emotion and experience that accompany the Christmas season in America. She disarms with simple and beautiful words, good humor, and a clear invitation to live into the complexity of being a human in this time and place. This book is a gift for anyone in the process of actively becoming more of who God made them to be, especially in the cacophony of pressures amid the holiday season."

—**Kate Reuer Welton**, Lutheran campus pastor, University of Minnesota–Twin Cities

"Treat yourself to a few moments of sacred wonder this holiday season with the help of Meta Herrick Carlson's delightful *Ordinary Blessings for the Christmas Season*. Meditating on the hidden joys of the everyday and reflecting on the deeper meaning of the characters and traditions of the season, Meta offers us an unvarnished and accessible Christmas with words of such simple beauty they will take your breath away."

—**David J. Lose**, senior pastor at Mount Olivet Lutheran Church, Minneapolis; former president of The Lutheran Theological Seminary at Philadelphia

"Sometimes tender, sometimes prickly, these blessings run the gamut from heartache and longing to giddy enthusiasm. Everything we know from the season—stories, words, and emotions—is addressed with unsentimental honesty, wry humor, and delighted expectation. These blessings make me want to enter into the Christmas season months ahead of time, just to ponder slowly all that the season holds."

—**Chad Winterfeldt**, cantor of Christ Chapel, Gustavus Adolphus College

"Meta Herrick Carlson has an unparalleled capacity to find the sacred in the daily and to grace everyday moments of life with beauty and humor in equal measure. She invites us to stop and notice that perhaps the ordinary is not so ordinary after all. This jewel of a book will quickly become a well-thumbed, 'ready to hand' book for parents, teachers, religious leaders, and more."

—**Rev. Dr. Chris Bellefeuille**, lead pastor of Trinity Lutheran Church, Stillwater, Minnesota

"Christmas: that convoluted season where 'merry and bright' looks a lot more like 'overworked and exhausted.' Never fear: Meta Herrick Carlson is here again, with another deeply true and deeply transformative book of blessings. Leave this one by the coffee maker and pick a random prayer each weary morning: you might find yourself feeling a little more 'joy to the world' after all."

—**Emmy Kegler**, author of *One Coin Found* and *All Who Are Weary*

"Meta Herrick Carlson gives balm for each aching joint in our holiday traditions with curiosity, wit, courage, and grace. From the raucous kids table to the chaotic checkout counter to the furtive chats about keeping to a budget, these incantations bless the mess and beckon the beautiful out of days made extraordinary by season and story. Each blessing broadens sacred traditions and sets our celebration tables with the fresh voice of emerging adults, the deep harmony of our elders, and the sparkle of our children. This book unwraps the tired, overstretched parent in me to welcome the youthful wonder that I don't quite deserve but that sneaks up nonetheless with the sticky fingers and twinkling smile of a toddler pulling down a beloved ornament from the tree. Thank you for finishing my Christmas shopping with this gift for everyone on my list."

—**Matthew Ian Fleming**, founding director
of Church Anew

Ordinary Blessings

for the
Christmas Season

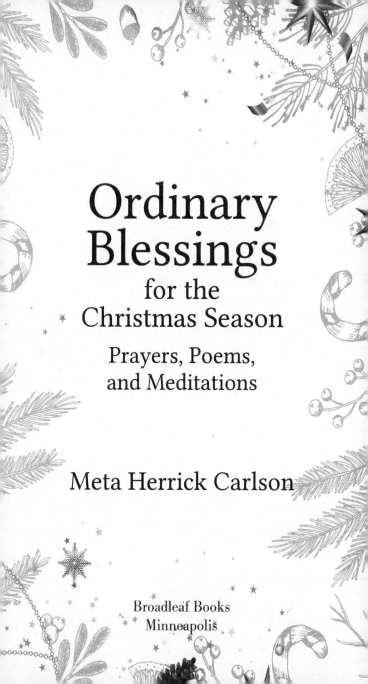

Ordinary Blessings
for the
Christmas Season

Prayers, Poems,
and Meditations

Meta Herrick Carlson

Broadleaf Books
Minneapolis

For my parents and brothers,
who feel like home everywhere
we go and no matter how we celebrate

Contents

※ ※ ※ ※ ※ ※ ※ ※ ※ ※ ※ ※

Blessings for Celebrating Christmas in a Church

Blessings for Families

Blessings for Holiday Grief

Blessings for Holiday Travel

Blessings for the Holiday Table

Blessings for Winter

**Blessings for the Ancient
Christmas Story**

Blessings for Each Day in Advent

Blessings for the Twelve Days of Christmas

Preface

The decorations are tucked inside one big storage bin that we haul out at the end of November. Sometimes we have the festive bandwidth for a roaring fire, a holiday playlist, or apple cider. I love to string up the garlands and paper chains they made as preschoolers. We clear a corner of the living room for the tree while the kids peruse ornaments with more nostalgia than their years warrant. It takes about an hour, and when we're finished, I look around and ruin the moment with a thought, "Maybe this year, we'll have our act together in time for Christmas."

I don't know where that vague pressure comes from or why it wants to make metrics for the season. Jesus is going to be born whether I'm ready or not. God is coming near because we need to be known and loved and saved up close.

Perfection and performance do not get the last word.

There is so much goodness in the small and simple things that surprise us, even while we're trying to get our act together. My role as a parish pastor means I get to see the sacred ordinary in the everyday lives and big life events of my community:

The Christmas Eve service was traditional, but the hymn singing before the service began was a ruckus of real time requests. People came early to make sure their favorite song, the tune that had been waiting in their lungs all year or might not be part of the worship service, would get an audience.

Grandma made a fancy Jell-O dessert every year, which the children politely tasted. But Grandpa made it silly and fun by tossing M&Ms into their dishes whenever his wife wasn't looking.

Mom had them posing all year for a decent picture on their holiday card, but in the end chose the chaotic one, when no one was ready for the shutter to click.

When their college student brought his friends home for winter break, they learned how to make dishes from Guatemala and China together. They set a bigger table that welcomed them home, even while they were far from home.

Dad made table place cards with pronouns and printed facts about chosen names from the internet, ready to educate anyone who needed help understanding why there would be new rules at his table this year.

The oldest had some ideas about Santa Claus, but kept them to herself for the sake of her younger sibling, who was full of magic and childlike wonder. She didn't mind believing a little longer.

The first Christmas without his partner would be too much to bear, so he downplayed the traditions and planned to spend the days alone. But their friends took turns showing up with food and games that conjured good memories and held space to remember his beloved in community.

The blessings in this collection recognize the holy stories and the sacred moments of the season. And they acknowledge what is tricky and troublesome about being in community during the holidays. May they take you to church and also meet you at home, a gentle reminder that you do not need to get your act together to receive what is already on the way.

God becomes flesh because your ordinary is worthy of divine interest, presence, and love. It will find you in the mess of consumerism and family drama and old stories you hear anew. May a phrase or blessing in this collection recognize the fullness of who you are and what you feel this Christmas season. And, since I'm no expert at this, I hope you'll join me in finding more words and ways to bless the ordinary.

BLESSINGS FOR
CELEBRATING CHRISTMAS
IN THE WORLD

For Writing a Christmas Letter

✳ ✳ ✳ ✳ ✳ ✳ ✳ ✳ ✳ ✳ ✳

This year has been flawed and full
in ways we cannot boil down
into pithy, fascinating, or funny.

But we try anyway, don't we?
Because it's one way to mark time
and make sense of everything
that's good and hard and true,
like telling it slant in under a page
will put the breaking and growing
in order, organized and notarized
by the distant approval of those we tell.

Remember, while you sit and stare
at the cursor blinking on an empty page,
that volumes cannot contain
the quiet miracles that came to pass.
And the postal service will never be able
to deliver a concise telling of
all the dying and rising of this wild and holy
and not-so-chronological year.

For Addressing Christmas Cards

✳ ✳ ✳ ✳ ✳ ✳ ✳ ✳ ✳ ✳ ✳

This is a time for remembering
people you hold dear
and the places they call home,
the chapters that brought you
together and the fondness
you feel even now, years later.

May these cards be sent
far and wide and generously
so that your thoughtful affection
finds their real lives
with reassurance that you recall
the nexus of this gladness.

FOR RECEIVING CHRISTMAS CARDS

Thank goodness for the days
this stack of mail contains
more merriment than payments due,
more stories and pictures
from a wide constellation of those
we squint to see more clearly
like light that travels time,
coming near with season's greetings.

This blessing extends to the rough edges,
the hard and sanded down parts
cropped and brightened to please,
a peace that's paper thin and easy to fold.

This blessing holds everything shared
with tender reverence for what remains
just out of view or between the lines,
the fullness for which God has come.

FOR MAIL CARRIERS

This blessing knows you mean it
when you say rain, sleet, or snow,
that you carry tidings of great joy
and the heavy distance between
hearts and hands, the space
we fill with seasonal sacraments,
the ingredients in each package
a word and an ordinary object
that become extraordinary when
it is sent and held with love.

For Mall Santas

For the Santas whose threadbare suits
smell like Santas from other shifts

For the Santas who rehearse their Ho Ho Hos
and still scare children plopped on their laps

For the Santas who ring bells at storefronts
or sit framed on more mantles than they know

For the Santas who hear both petty greed
and heart-wrenching grief whispered into their
    ears

For the Santas who Santa because they have
    seen
how much the magic matters every single year.

For Retail Workers

✳ ✳ ✳ ✳ ✳ ✳ ✳ ✳ ✳ ✳ ✳ ✳

For every sentimental and thoughtful purchase,
you are an innocent bystander to the hurried
     mess
of our consumption and reckless want of things.

You might be the first to admit that money can't
     buy
what we are restless to satisfy,
and still, you help us find what we're seeking.

You are there while we curate gifts and plan
     meals,
privy to our motivations and moods with
     overtures
of gift wrap and patience we might not deserve.

When you are tending to your own preparations,
may you receive the gracious assistance and
     care
you have shown: a sincere tribute to the season.

FOR FIFTH GRADE BAND CONCERTS

✳ ✳ ✳ ✳ ✳ ✳ ✳ ✳ ✳ ✳ ✳

The audience is a roster
of invested superfans
and one eager grandfather
who is beyond proud
that a knack for the trombone
lives on in another generation.

Younger siblings have been bribed
with simple carbs to withstand
the test of the full program event,
though it may prove a tall order.

There are more F sharps
than we bargained for.

When the crowd finds the melody,
they join the beat with their bodies
and hum, just hoping it helps.

The band teacher conducts
with baton, brow, and beads of sweat,
face resolved with a grimacing smile
that is grace to cover every student in love.

The band is learning and so are we.
They are trying to be brave in public,
to make something beautiful together.

FOR UNCOMFORTABLE CLOTHES

✳ ✳ ✳ ✳ ✳ ✳ ✳ ✳ ✳ ✳ ✳

There are a few hours this season
when we must peel off and fold neatly
with deep reverence the three pairs
of stretchy pants we've worn in a tidy rotation.

When the event requires something more,
this blessing goes with you to the closet.
It will stand watch while you sigh
thoughtfully at the options available.

It will nod in support while you lay out clothes
for small children they have never seen
and do not plan to wear willingly.

It has weathered battles over itchy tags
and limp clip-on bow ties and high-water slacks.

These moments are unfortunate at best
and performative at worst, so when you can,
wear something that feels like you
and remember you are already beautiful.

Eat the meal. Take the picture. Chat away.
And trust your leisurewear is waiting for you.

FOR DECORATING THE TREE

Ornaments are stories,
signs and symbols of ways
you have claimed and collected
a world onto branches that call
this hallowed room home.

May scribbles and popsicle sticks
find places of honor alongside
fine tokens and treasures,
together making the room bigger
and brighter than it was before.

FOR WHEN THEY ASK ABOUT SANTA

❋ ❋ ❋ ❋ ❋ ❋ ❋ ❋ ❋ ❋ ❋

There is a spirit at work
in this season of plenty
that lingers just beyond
the logic of little ones.

However they ask,
and however you tell,
fold them into the magic
that moves through generations,
that declares every single child
worthy of miracles, a generous story,
and love that calls them good.

FOR WRAPPING PRESENTS

✳ ✳ ✳ ✳ ✳ ✳ ✳ ✳ ✳ ✳ ✳

I wait until it's late at night
to spread out all the supplies
on the living room floor,
under the soft glow of twinkle lights
and a TV show I'm hardly watching.

The dog is snoring
until he hears me cut the paper,
and now he thinks we're playing a game.

We are not playing a game.
This is serious business.

I get up several more times—
the ratio of labels and bows is always off,
and the clear plastic tape never lasts.

What gets assembled before it's wrapped?
Does Santa get his own color of paper?
Who thought glitter was a good idea?

But then it is finished,
and they are stacked like mysteries,
spilling out from under the tree,
and I can't help but stare and marvel
at the already and not yet.

Blessings for
Celebrating Christmas
in a Church

For Trying to Get to Church on Time

They say the hour before arriving
at worship is the most ungodly hour
for parents of small children.

But then again, in the house of God,
the maker of heaven and earth,
the one who was, who is, who is to come,
what is time, anyway?

This blessing is hoping you don't get
all the wheels screwed back on before
you find a pew so that you will bring more
of your wobbly selves inside.

Do not portion yourself as an offering
but rather trust Jesus when he tells the crowds,
"No one knows the day or the hour, not even
   the Son."

FOR THOSE WHO ONLY COME
TO CHURCH ON CHRISTMAS

There is an ancient refrain,
an invitation to come and see.
And whether the call sounds
like a dare or directive,
it does not really matter.

Come and see the flames
dancing on your neighbor's face.

Come and see little children
squirming and curious, hearts
wide open to magic and mystery.

Come and see the wax
melting down your fingertips,
giving itself away to the light
warm and changing.

Come and see a room
filled with hope for love
that catches us up and keeps us,
tonight and every night,
now until the end of time.

FOR SANCTUARY DECORATIONS

Evergreen, candlelight, and crèche
come out of storage,
dusty remnants polished clean,
and the space awakens with
simple symbols of what can't wait—
the God who flourishes,
who shines in the darkness,
who makes a home among us,
declaring our ordinary
good enough all over again.

FOR THE CHILDREN'S
CHRISTMAS PROGRAM

This story has been told so many ways,
by Matthew and Luke, by children and choirs,
with flubs and forgotten lines that amplify
what is gorgeous and uncontainable
about God getting so close to our mortality,
to our trying and failing and trying some more.

There is room in the story for big yawns,
for the patina of musty costume accessories
and little ones singing so softly you can only
hear the choir director and a pin drop.

Watch Mary sneer at Joseph and wonder
about everything we cannot know for sure.
Give thanks for their bodies learning
to hold the story, to know that love is here.

FOR BELOVED CHRISTMAS HYMNS

Advent was brief and flew away
with one, maybe two renditions.

Christmas is for all the verses,
a chorus of people gathered in
by forces of faith unseen, preaching
Joy to the World and Silent Night.

Christmas is for anthems that wait
all year long in the dark depths
of our lungs for a time such as this,
to revive the world with hope that sings.

FOR CHURCH EMPLOYEES

This blessing knows you worship
in the shadows of setup and cleanup,
in the milliseconds between tasks
and mental notes made for next year.

You know magic in the fullness
of what you plan and what falls apart,
in the sights and sounds too beautiful
to be anything but God's own doing.

The miracle is for you too, Beloved.
There is faithfulness in letting go
and trusting that Christ will be born,
no matter what you do or leave undone.

For When Faith Has Changed

The story of Christmas is wide,
for it gathers in and sends out
the last and least expected.

Make generous room at the inn
and ready the barn for a whole host
of visitors, gifts, and anthems.

Follow the star and dream big
about the ways God continues
to speak and dwell among us.

Recall how often in scripture
the good news and the truest thing
came first to the margins.

Recognize that being centered,
steeped in familiar ways, can make it harder
to see God stirring on the edges,
and a gentle reminder to keep moving
toward awe can be the greatest gift of all.

BLESSINGS FOR FAMILIES

FOR SCHEDULING
FAMILY CELEBRATIONS

Blessed are they who make and keep plans,
who find a reliable pattern that sticks and feels
   mutual.

Blessed are they who compare fluid calendars
around shift work and worship, budgets and
   travel,
due dates and depression and inpatient
   treatment.

Blessed are they who let others decide and go
   with the flow,
who bring some perspective and mediate well.

Blessed are they who leave the text thread
because they are saving their patience for the
   main event,
who do not need to be in the know to love you
   well.

For Negotiating Who
Will Celebrate Where

This is not exactly a hostage negotiation,
because we are willing participants year after
 year.

Nor is it an NFL draft with rules and pomp
that decide your fate for better or worse.

There are several interested parties involved,
and so we reach out each fall to decide together:

What does it look like this year?
How do we come together or compromise?
Whose expectations will be met or dashed?

May we listen deeply in the planning, so we
 know
what needs to be honored in the celebration:

Babies and budgets. Work shifts and worship.
Pronouns and partners and privacy.

May we listen deeply in the planning, so we
 know
it is different every single time and
it is a beautiful privilege every single time.

FOR BABY'S FIRST CHRISTMAS

✳ ✳ ✳ ✳ ✳ ✳ ✳ ✳ ✳ ✳ ✳

You cannot begin to know, Little One,
how this story has come alive and anew
in our hearts and arms this year.

We are like Joseph, traveling home
to be counted and dreaming up plans.

We are like Mary, receiving treasure
and pondering everything in our hearts.

We are like shepherds, washing our hands
and leaning in for a good and holy look.

We are like a barnyard, messy space
overtaken by you and fresh belonging.

For Trying to Make Everybody Happy

So how is it going,
the straining and striving
to make sure others
get to stay comfortable
so they don't have to
imagine a wholeness beyond
the annual preservation
and preference of a few?

Remember that when you fail
to make everybody happy,
you have succeeded in damaging
the routine that holds you back.
You are one error closer
to experiencing joy yourself,
and the discovery of another way
forward for the whole.

For Drawing a Line in the Sand

✸ ✸ ✸ ✸ ✸ ✸ ✸ ✸ ✸ ✸ ✸

When you have been crystal clear
and held boundaries that matter,
but the arrows keep flying
laced with poison you're trying to quit,

go ahead and get loud
about the space you need to be whole,
the distance that will keep you safe
and recover your full humanity.

You do not owe anyone
hearty chunks of yourself
just because someone else
decided their expectations are final.

When you know in your body
that this pressure is not Christmas,
remember the inn is not the only place
to believe and belong and birth tonight.

This blessing will help you draw the line
with grief and mercy, and even hope
if it means you get to be your whole self
and experience love incarnate elsewhere.

For When You Don't Have the Kids This Year

There are things to be missed this time,
sacred moments stretched long distance,
hollowed out and stiff with quiet grief
when they aren't right here to react in time.

Tie a blessing to what they pack
woven in and around their little wares,
a tangled thread of love that stretches
to cover the space between here and there.

And keep one in the folds of your soft waiting,
a word that knows what's hard and good
that reminds you true love is made flesh
and they carry you with them, even now.

For Adult Children
Hosting for the First Time

There are a lot of ways to honor
what has already been,
traditions that shaped you and
elders who taught you to gather.

May your space and your style
host a spirit of gratitude for these things
without contention or copy, but
joyful exploration of your provision.

For Relatives
We Don't See Often

When we don't see one another
often enough to settle into a rhythm,
a mutual expectation for time spent
and roles played, it requires a bit of
remembering, reminding, and reconnecting.

The clumsy creation of this routine is not
a commentary on the devotion present here.

Rather it is a testament to the love that wills us
together for tender and curious trying.

When we don't see one another
often enough to settle into a rhythm,
it leaves room for the characters
to grow and change, for resetting the table
with sight for all things being made new.

FOR BEFORE YOU GO INSIDE

Before you go inside,
put one hand on your heart.
Wait with your body and listen
to the blood that pumps
out through your body
and back to your core.

Remember that you are
being brave and then
coming home to yourself
quietly and fiercely and all the time.

Before you go inside,
hold the soft of your belly.
Breathe with your body and feel
how full you become
when you are taking up space
and holding life in your lungs.

Remember that you are
drawing in what is good, and then
letting go what is finished,
quietly and fiercely and all the time.

BLESSINGS FOR
HOLIDAY GRIEF

FOR THE FIRST CHRISTMAS WITHOUT THEM

This season has been
a hundred thousand firsts
without them, every breath
a reminder that they do not
breathe this air anymore,

every story of incarnation
a reminder that they are not
embodied in flesh anymore,

every song or meal or party
a reminder of the things
they loved this time of year

every ad selling quality time
with the ones you love
a reminder it cannot be bought

every word of hope is sour,
a bitter flavor that reminds you
how long ago it tasted sweet.

FOR DEPRESSION

We could call it the winter blues,
claim that the cold darkness alters
energy and mood, and they probably do.

We could say the forced merriment
is a little much or make some assumptions
about the social tolerance for these things.

But this is also a chemically induced despair,
a cellar that cannot perform at ground level
or pretend according to objective urging.

The world may demand hope all it likes,
but not from this crypt of anguish.

Do not ask of me according to the impatient
annoyance and discomfort of this world.

Rather, ask the One who knows what it's like
to be both mortal and God, bound and free.

Ask the One who has been to the end
of everything and comes back so we can live.

For Substance Abuse

There is a chasm that keeps us
waiting, grieving, holding our breath
for an expatriate we try so hard
to summon and re-member with
hazy and hopeful memories.

It sounds a little like Advent . . .
or perhaps occupation and exile.

It feels like a tough ratio
of judgment and mercy from
every prophet, including the ones
who don't say anything out loud.

It looks like resenting the remnant
until the space in between is so wide
even our cautious descriptions
of benign and beautiful things
struggle to preserve what's left
of the breath we keep holding.

For When We Don't
Talk about That

May the concessions we outgrow
be deemed null and void
by newfound curiosity and courage.

May the secrets we hold close
belong to those who deserve our trust,
whose safety and power are righteous.

May the things we hold back
be left unsaid because of patient love
rather than performance and pleasing.

May the truth about what is off the table
be made clear for every generation so
descendants can decide for themselves.

For When Your Welcome
Is Conditional

The kingdom of heaven is like
a welcome in which your wholeness
and your neighbors' wholeness
do not conflict but compound,
where your safety does not depend on
the personal comfort of others
but basks in the generous delight
that God has for your real life,
your healed self, and your identity as
beloved without a single condition.

FOR TERMINAL TENSION

This scene is fractured light,
a kaleidoscope of memories
that spins slowly around so
it's hard to see the one picture
you want my focus to catch,
the pose you want me to take.

It's hidden inside everything,
dancing distracting distorting
how long we have been telling
completely different stories,
this strain held weary but taut
with no sign or reason for slack.

For When There Isn't Enough Therapy

We can only do our own work, which
might not feel like enough these days.

Blessed are those who can't or won't,
who say they totally do, but probably don't.

Blessed are those who are trying,
and those who have stopped trying too.

Blessed are those who have their hands full
with their own breaking and mending.

Blessed are those who are learning to voice
what they need and decline without explanation.

Blessed are those who teach us to heal,
who will get an earful at appointments in
    January.

For When You Need a Christmas Miracle

Set this blessing
slender and sturdy
like a candle in the window,
watching and waiting,
shining so someone
will see and believe
that little things can matter
a lot, and miracles can look like
love that's paying attention.

For Infertility at Christmas

✳ ✳ ✳ ✳ ✳ ✳ ✳ ✳ ✳ ✳ ✳

I do not rejoice with Mary,
who is foolish and favored,
both maiden and mother,
idealized for centuries
as the perfect paradox
of a woman—a fertile virgin.

I loathe this season that
simplifies what has been
painstakingly difficult and cruel,
magnifies what has been
so uncertain and songless,
domesticates what has been
wild, hormonal, expensive,
and pricked with despair each time
I am reminded she has a due date
while I am left to wonder
not when but if ever.

FOR A SHOESTRING BUDGET

✳ ✳ ✳ ✳ ✳ ✳ ✳ ✳ ✳ ✳ ✳

When what you have
is thin and threaded through
every purchase and promise
you make and muster,
wrap this blessing like aglets
at each end of your cord
so it can stretch and lace
with a little less fear and fray,
so you can touch it and
feel your own resilience,
that you are more than enough,
miraculous, double knotted, and true.

Blessings for
Holiday Travel

For Travelers

We have long been on the move
toward home and family
or freedom and love—
or sometimes,
to our own great surprise,
all of these things.

The listening strains longer,
beneath the logistics and
restlessness of public journey.

Here our bodies remember
migration is innately human
and pilgrimage is an ancient
calling to remind us we are home
even if we are far from home.

FOR LONG CAR RIDES

There is time on the way
for coming home to yourself,
for recognizing
what is hard and good about
attending these gatherings,
what is true no matter where you are.

Make playlists that preach
stories of loss and love and life,
an album to sing of past and present.

Pack snacks that set a table
on the way to more formal feasts,
that grant comfort for the drive.

Keep watch and stay awake,
Advent's holy directives,
all the way there and back again.

For Driving on Icy Roads

That old song about
a horse drawn sleigh
navigating river and woods
to Grandmother's house
didn't say anything
about black ice and low visibility.

But here we are in modern vehicles,
creeping through winter's worst,
just hoping to show up on time
and in one piece, praying
we can muster some holiday cheer
upon arrival when cell service
allows a lone message through:

*Can you pick up some half-and-half
on your way, if it's not too much trouble?*

FOR FLIGHT ATTENDANTS

Blessed are those
who welcome aboard
and go with us in the interest of
our adventure and not their own,
who labor on their feet,
who trade common courtesy
for pretzels and rail drinks
while we sit back and experience
the miracle of flight
like it's nothing but an inconvenience
on the way from here to there.

For a Delayed
or Canceled Flight

I'm pretending to hold it together
because I want to be perceived
as a decent person in this mass
of people equally inconvenienced.

I'm pretending to hold it together,
but the dominos are already falling,
and this means missing connections,
not to mention my sense of order.

I'm pretending to hold it together,
but this was going to be the part of the trip
when I just went through the motions
while furtively switching gears internally.

I'm pretending to hold it together
because I'm not ready to be disappointed
by plans changed and needs unmet,
or the logistics too tender to tend.

For Waiting for Loved Ones to Arrive

The haste and hustle
of time spent preparing slows
until the watch feels unreasonable,
the long anticipation rising
like butterflies in your stomach
the fever of your voice.

When there is nothing left to do
but wait, sink into the meaning
of these incarnate holy weeks,
the sound of your heart beating
between already and not yet,
the tenderness of almost here.

FOR HOMEGOING

I did not recognize
the tightness in my body
until the Spirit whispered,
"You don't have to go back
yet. Or ever."

No need to stuff it all back
inside so it counts or continues,
so some are satisfied when
you are more and there is room
to bloom out here.

Blessings for the
Holiday Table

FOR A SEAT AT THE TABLE

I hope you eat or do not eat
something on your own terms,
because you are delicious.

I hope you are asked about
your life unlaced from expectations,
because you are fascinating.

I hope you have plenty of elbow room
and someone for glances and grins,
because you are good company.

I hope you come and go as one
who is loved and whole and free.

For Harvest

Every year I try to grow
too many things that need
more space than the distance,
at which I plant them in raised beds
that prove no match
for the dog's vegetarian impulse.

Every year I manufacture shade
a few weeks too late or go out of town
and forget to ask a neighbor to water
the bursts of leaves and vines
that have already decided a yield
for themselves and without my input.

Every year there is an abundance
of something and a lack of something else
so that I must find neighbors with whom
I can offer my plenty and ask for help,
and practice learning to trust that
the harvest is beautiful and best shared.

For Passing On a Beloved Family Recipe

The card is worn thin,
seedy and soiled
with the same ingredients
listed on her lines,
in faded cursive
that tells the story of a person
who made good
food with big love.

Full-color cardstock copies
save the messy flare
and laminate each one
to preserve the old marks,
passing them out
after dinner so this spell
will live another generation
and take on a life of its own.

For Embracing New Foods When You Marry into a Family

There is room on every table
for what you need not try
and for what you are willing to risk.

Food is fuel, sure. And it is also love
of culture and elders and senses.

May your introduction to customs here
be given as invitation and not command,
never questioning your place at the table.

And may the way this food is shared
allow for more boards and chairs added
for newcomers inside our legends and lore.

For the Kids' Table

Rowdy and set apart,
the youngest gaggle,
counting one fun uncle
sent for the sake of
humor and supervision,
and half hiding out
where he feels at home.

Once the runt of the litter
and now the king, able
to cut his own meat
and steer the conversation
until it's silly and sacred,
and all the grown-ups are
a little jealous of the kids' table.

For Different Diets

Thank goodness
there are a thousand ways
to make potatoes delectable
so everyone can find a dish
that tastes like welcome.

Varied servings and choices,
a constellation of bright scents
and signs to illumine your place
at a living feast, a table set anew
and satisfaction each time.

Coming together
around different diets
is one way we practice consent,
honoring our bodies and trusting
each other to theirs, too.

For a Cookie Exchange

This is a recipe for people and gathering,
for a variety that makes for
a sacramental quorum of friendship.

Two coordinators who take turns
in the modest competition of keeping
what was and enfolding the new.

One who is spicy and salty,
who comes with storebought dough
because their gift is in the air they bring.

One who records the years in recipes,
on notecards or in a shared document
as memory keeper for the whole.

One who doesn't bake but hosts,
who spends the day looking forward
to cleaning their own enormous kitchen.

One who is invited and means to come,
but who never does, and still they are invited
because some of us are fed by the ask.

One who points out they never come
and that maybe it's time to update the list,
who says what a few might be thinking.

One who gently reminds the one and the whole
that sometimes we need a safe place to say no,
where we won't be canceled and loved even still.

One who makes the cookies everyone wants,
who makes more than their fair share
because this is who they are and what they do.

FOR SOBRIETY

It feels dangerous
to keep all my wits about me,
to feel the full tenderness
of my skin and senses humming
to a full symphony of presence.
I haven't allowed myself to play
up and against the holiday crooners
and clinking glassware and chitchat
of these familiar and fuzzy rituals.

It feels dangerous
to take off my mask, the one I wore
for them but mostly for myself,
so that I am suddenly participating
like an understudy called up to see
how well I know the lines
and what I might bring to the part,
a truth that's been missing for a while.

It feels dangerous
because it is dangerous.
I am dangerous whenever
I am practicing how to be free.

For Leftovers

Stuffed and sleepy after dinner,
we put the wishbone near the sink
and pack away the leftover meat
in mismatched Tupperware,
convinced we can't eat another bite,
let alone look at it.

But then it comes back out
as cold nibbles and reheated plates,
in sandwiches and soups,
as salads if we get creative.
It keeps, even after the bone
dries and breaks and wishes come true.

For Cleaning the Kitchen

❋ ❋ ❋ ❋ ❋ ❋ ❋ ❋ ❋ ❋ ❋

When you have used every place setting
and serving bowl you own,

when the stovetop is decorated
with sauce that splashed and crust that dried,

when you can't tell which towels are clean
and where to start clearing surface area,

take a moment to admire the mess you made,
the mouths fed and the bellies filled,
the ones you collected for this feast,
and the symptoms of this meal's success.

And then start calling out orders, recruiting
    help,
and hosing it down to prepare for the next time
they all come around to taste and see what is
    good.

BLESSINGS FOR WINTER

For Autumn Anguish

I know what is broken.
It rouses raw regrets
in the dark frost of night.

It waits with me, haunting
the stories I tell myself until
dawn breaks its power.

It will be back at dusk.
I have these hours to catch
my breath in the sun's soft glow.

She is trying so hard, too,
rising just above tree line
with a weary smile that knows

this light is not enough, and still
what she brings is everything.

For Winter Clothes Outgrown

✳ ✳ ✳ ✳ ✳ ✳ ✳ ✳ ✳ ✳ ✳

The plastic bin barely closed last spring
and bursts open with little help now
that crisp air and rumors of weather
and notes from the schoolteacher
suggest having all the gear ready
for the inevitable, just in case.

I could have sworn these things
were all washed and folded,
that every mitten had a friend,
that some things had been donated
or handed down to smaller cousins already,
but this mess of puffy layers
still smells like a sweaty snow day,
the capri-length, camel-toe snow pants
mock my sense of how fast these kids grow,
and mock the kids, too, while they wear
mismatched remnants of last year
for these first and false start weeks of winter.

FOR EARLY DUSK

The days fold in on themselves
this time of year, shorter and softer
than things we have planned,
peaking early with a knowing
that is both firm and gentle,
with a kindness that reminds creatures
we are called to a few things,
but not all the things all at once.

For the Color of Permission

✳ ✳ ✳ ✳ ✳ ✳ ✳ ✳ ✳ ✳ ✳

The darkness spreads
wide enough to cover the
commutes and gathering posts,
our plans for going out and coming in.

Neighbors become strangers
in the hustle of dawn and dusk,
our transitions disguised and apart
while we bundle in layers of wool.

The light is reluctant and brief,
like it can't wait to go back to bed,
like it was never awake, not really.
To say it's been shining is a stretch.

To say I've been shining is a stretch.
So I watch the pink afternoon sky
and decide this is the color of permission
I didn't know I needed until just now.

FOR A BROWN CHRISTMAS

People of the North, how you grieve
a Christmas without snow!

How you long for a blanket of cold
white powder to cover the sleeping earth,

to brighten what is hard and harsh
about this frigid and forbidding climate.

If it makes you feel any better,
Baby Jesus had a brown Christmas.

It was probably chilly, the crisp air
piercing through his swaddling clothes.

But snow for sleigh rides
and sledding was not in the forecast.

And still, love was born anyway.

For First Flurries

This blessing knows you are busy
trying to make magic this season
by hiding presents and filling stockings,
stringing lights and hanging ornaments
that whisper local and sacred stories
and smell of evergreen and promises

but do not miss the magic that blows
like air fronts colliding, like clouds
turning out ice crystals that tumble down
and swirl both separate and en masse,
dancing and delivering the wonder
that comes easily to seasons turning.

FOR SHOVELING

Begin bundled up since
it will be impossibly cold
until suddenly it isn't

until the sure rhythm of
hard scrapes and soft silence
warm your blood, rendering
scarf and gloves useless

until you begin to marvel
at your hearty grit
and embrace your own speed
because there is no rush

until the piles prepared rise high
like mountains of childhood memories
frigid fortresses that conjure
something wild in your blood

until it is pumping so hard
your pulse becomes another layer
in the clearing of space and snow,
in the clearing of your winter mind.

For Winter Solstice

This is permission to burrow
to hide in the warm simplicity of
a dark cave
of gratitude and belonging.

Do not let the demands of the world
inside today. There is only a little light
enough to cast a glow on
what is actually necessary.

It is a sabbath encore, however short
to let God mind the world while it is soaked
in the cold, dark exposure that begs
for a sign of life after death.

For Hibernation

There is a hope chest in the basement
filled with cedar chips and old quilts,
patches of old-fashioned patterns that sleep
while we sun in the warmth of the world
until the windows close and the heat kicks on
and chords of wood are chopped and stored.

We summon those layers of love to rise
when the frost sticks to windowpanes
and the hearth heats, to cover and keep us
in the warm glow of one another,
hunkered down like a den of bears,
heartbeats slow and trusting slumber's gift.

FOR BARE BRANCHES

Do not measure yourself by
things done and left undone,
no matter what the shadows say.

You are brave and bare branches,
gnarled and eerie at dusk,
stunning in the crisp air of dawn.

You are a sprig that shoots out
even after everything is cut down,
nervy and reaching anyway.

The exposure is beautiful,
you're not enough and you're everything.
Be revealed as you are and shine.

Today is short and not yet written.

FOR LONG NIGHTS

It can feel lonely
when this side of the earth
is tipped outward, turned
into the chaos and void,
the warmth of other stars
many light years away.

It can sound like silence
when we wake several times
during the night expecting
dawn (surely by now!),
only to find more darkness
and time standing still.

It can look forgotten
when long shadows linger
all day and night, tenebrosity
that covers every living thing
with more patience than we
could conjure on our own.

For Wind Chill

❋ ❋ ❋ ❋ ❋ ❋ ❋ ❋ ❋ ❋

Wear this blessing
like a gator that tucks in,
way down under the collar
of your coat and into layers,
pulled up around your face
at angles that guard
your neck and ears
your cheeks and nose so that
only your eyes are left to witness
the arid front charging toward you
with conviction and might
that refuses to be tamed,
gusts of formidable force
that cannot break you, either.

For Clear Skies

Sometimes when it is clear and cold,
I step outside and look way up
to see heaven's banner stretching,
expansive and exploding,
to remember and honor
the ancestors and ancient dreams,
everything that came before
and the light that is still coming
to guide travelers and kindle visions
of heaven's splendor near and now.

FOR THAW

Listen.
The earth is melting
like a deep sigh,
relaxing her shoulders,
drinking in everything
that has been waiting
to fill and nourish
her dormant depths,
the haunts of her roots
and secret desires
that will rise with color
and a tenacious will
that cannot stay dead
for long.

BLESSINGS FOR THE
ANCIENT CHRISTMAS STORY

FOR A KING

The people said,
We want a king just like
all the other nations.

Samuel took this personally,
but God reassured him,
They are not rejecting you—
they are rejecting me.
Listen to the people. And also
remind them about kings.

So he listened. And then
he spoke hard truth with big love:

Kings put their own interests first
and make your children servants
in fields and on front lines.

Kings require a measure
of your security for their pleasure
so that many live and die
according to the whims of a few.

But the people already knew this
and were set on a king anyway.

Inspired by 1 Samuel: 8

For the Four Women
in Jesus's Family Tree

If God wished to be born
into perfection and peace,
we'd still be waiting
on a Savior of the world.

God knows families are messy,
that our generations
are full of characters,
our stories told slant with time.

And so the Word of God
is tangled up with DNA
of those familiar and forgotten,
heroes and villains and ordinary folks,

heartache and faithful promises,
tales of courage and cowardice
woven through a patriarchy
interrupted by four women

trusted by God to break the rules
when rules were wrong,
to act for liberation and love
that made a way for even more.

Inspired by Matthew 1

For Zechariah

It's one thing
to take your voice for granted,
and it's quite another
to think you know the plan,
to hold fast and tight
to what you deem possible
in the house of the Lord.

When he questioned the angel
for proof of promises,
the old priest was silenced.

Though perhaps the quiet
was never meant to punish,
for in the sabbatical of silence
and trimesters of contemplation
he grew into a gift for hearing
blessings and songs and new life,
impossibilities everywhere.

FOR ELIZABETH

She flings wide the door
and saunters outside
to bless her little cousin
to announce what is already true
to add her delight to God's
and celebrate how good it feels
to embody the impossible
and take up space in the story.

She opens her arms wide
so they can embrace with
shoulders, bellies, and voices
that bear witness to how much
God trusts women to carry
what is dangerous and holy
for the sake of generations
still forming inside us all.

FOR JOHN

He blazed a trail into the wild places
away from the center of status quo,
the restraint and preservation of holiness
a weathered sense of how it had to be.

He cried out with a voice that dared
to prepare a way into the unknown
for the One they'd been waiting on
for things they could not imagine all alone.

He was the beloved son of an old priest
who preferred temples among the trees
and washing in rivers to the pomp
of what had already been tried and true.

He stood between one age and the next,
called fool and nuisance and threat since
his is strange and humble work in a world
of folks who would rather be the One.

For Joseph

This blessing wonders about a father
who does not get a spoken word
and declares love incarnate anyway

about his code of honor and shame,
norms weighed by drama and duty
to keep him in line and deciding quietly

about a man who couldn't imagine
a future in which they belonged to each other
until a dream interrupted what he knew

about a partner who brought her home
and a parent who saved his newborn son,
a servant who believed dreams come true.

For Mary, Mother of Jesus

✳ ✳ ✳ ✳ ✳ ✳ ✳ ✳ ✳ ✳ ✳

Every year folks with the,
"Mary Did You Know?"

Yeah, she knew. An angel told her.

She opted in without asking
for permission from her father
or quietly convincing her fiancé.

She sang an earth-shaking prophecy
and had (stretch marked) skin in the game.

She knew. She super knew!

Her youth and virginity paint
our telling of Mary as vulnerable and mild.

But do not forget God's favor
for her power and good courage.
It has been there all along.

For Shepherds

This blessing keeps watch
with the ones who work
in the fourth watch and late nights,
who fight wolves and skip showers
and love God's creatures by name.

This blessing keeps watch
with the ones we take for granted,
who center the outskirts and
feel stormy weather in their joints,
who are often the last to hear

but the first when news is this good.

For Angels

Perhaps they looked like cherubs,
like pageant children dressed
in tinsel and tulle and white robes
with voices so sweet and pure
the shepherds sighed and smiled.

But I'd like to think they frightened
those men out of their own skin,
roaring in octaves foreign and fierce
creatures with talons and wings
more curious than any beast on earth.

I'd like to think they proclaimed
good news that shook the whole field,
a haunting pronouncement that
God in flesh would be untamable
and the world was already turning.

For Magi

Just when we think
we have a handle on
the boundaries of a blessing
a timeline worth trusting
the full setting
of a scene and story

witnesses arrive
with scents and sage
from so far off we can't
make sense of how they knew
or why they came
all this way to worship

so we make room for magic
receiving the gifts with grace
pondering these things
in the depths of our hearts
and changed by the scope of love
and another road home.

For Herod

Every story needs a villain,
an insecure imposter
who weaponizes family
and tries to cauterize a faith
to keep a throne he shouldn't have,
to retain power he borrowed
and stole with the blood
of everyone he could have loved.

Every story needs a villain,
so we must remember
who we do not wish to become
and who we might become anyway,
who we are just a little bit already,
and that we need saving from ourselves.

For Bethlehem's Babies

Their fate is just a footnote
in the annals of a story
so fiercely committed to birth,
the wonder and vulnerability
of a new generation rising together.

The jealous rage of one man
is enough to bring a town to its knees,
to hollow the hearts and wombs of mothers
whose lamentation and lactation rage
for their sons who are no more.

There is One who lives, who knows
how hard the powers of this world still try
to break the love that is breaking fear,
who weeps and waits with us,
who remembers the unforgettable.

For Saint Nicholas

He reigned as bishop
among those who had no one
in their corner; the silenced,
the stolen and sold.

Nicholas filled shoes with citrus
and tossed coins through windows
into stockings where children
did not know safety or love.

Do not be fooled by his title
or his fancy church hat.
Saint Nick still roams
righting wrongs after dark,
making magic and leaving mercy
in his wake.

For Saint Lucia

Legend says,
she wanted to give
her dowry to the poor.

Her mother urged her
to marry well and wait
to bequest funds at the end
of a safe and comfortable life.

But her privilege stirred
and she could not wait
until later to be generous.

So she fed the ones
who were hidden and afraid.
They say she avoided
a marriage match by
gouging out her eyes.

Her story traveled north
from Sicily to Sweden, where
people already knew the beauty
of light dancing in darkness and
the stewardship of right now.

For Our Lady of Guadalupe

✳ ✳ ✳ ✳ ✳ ✳ ✳ ✳ ✳ ✳ ✳

She appeared to him, a woman
who spoke Nahuatl and clearly,
so there could be no mistaking
that this was divine love in his midst.

She appeared to him, a woman
who introduced herself even though
she was already familiar
to his faithful spirit and self.

She appeared to him, a woman
who chose a peasant to echo
her prophetic song about joy and dignity
for the lowly and humble of heart.

She appeared to him, a woman
to gently chide and cheer him to action
with maternal love both soft and strong:
¿No estoy yo aquí que soy tu madre?

She appeared to him, a woman
who colored the hills with flowers in winter
and set her face upon his cloak
so all could see his story was true.

Blessings for Each
Day in Advent

Wonder

It is no small thing
to be surprised by
the sudden admiration
of a pleasant scene
set in a moment beyond
your own control.

May something
about this season
cause you to step back,
to shift your whole weight
while you take in the fullness
of what is still possible
so your gaze is bent by cosmic time
and the sneaking suspicion
that, in the end,
beauty needs no explanation.

LOVE

There is room this season
for every kind of love.

May your commitment and duty,
your faithful and familial love be honored.

May your passion and pleasure,
your affection and playfulness be honored.

May your intimacy and boundaries,
your sense of self-care and space be honored.

May your cosmic and expansive love,
your place within the order of things be
    honored.

May your love reflect God's rapture and
    devotion
for you and your whole life.

STAR

Blink and wait
for your eyes to adjust
to the night's sky
the dark embrace
of a universe stretching
from beginning until forever.

Receive the light
that traveled far and long
to meet your gaze
in this time and place,
to show you fire, dust, magic
ancient signs still coming true.

The cosmos is bright
for navigation and mystery.
She shines as if to say
every generation is worthy of light
to guide us into deep love
and home by another way.

PEACE

It is dangerous to pray for peace,
to ask God to reveal and unravel
our posture and pretending for
a semblance of love and justice.

It is dangerous to pray for peace
when we benefit from tumult unseen
and games rigged by earthly powers.

It is dangerous to pray for peace
when we fear our own fullness and life.

DELIGHT

Every revolution requires
a deliberate pursuit of joy,
the public practice of pleasure
and well-being that reminds us
why we resist Empire's despair
and strain for the Kingdom on earth.

Joy does not manifest all on its own,
nor can it be manufactured
by the clever wills of creation.

Rather it bubbles up, spilling out
from an ancient aquifer,
the deep source of Jacob's well,
the seas stirred up in Genesis,
the Spirit waters that have been
saving since the beginning.

This is Delight, the wellspring
of our original and eternal blessing:
good and very good, God's pleasure
alive in our breath and bodies,
sacred fuel for revolutions of love.

PREPARE

There is no going back
to the way things were,
but rather a call to notice

which tools can be
set down for awhile
distributed again
given freely
or left to rust in piles
of what is now finished.

Do not be rushed back
into old systems that
cannot begin to contain
what is still coming.

HOME

There is One who journeys
all the way here to live with us,
who finds unlikely refuge
in mangers and mother's breast,
in foreign exile and Temple,
who watches foxes in holes
and wonders aloud whether
he has a place in this world,
who shakes the dust off his sandals
and breaks bread as a guest,

whose breath is broken
by the powers of this world
that tell him to stay in the grave,
that he belongs only to death,

who rises to announce
his love for this world and a plan
to make his body a home
on heaven and earth for all
who are hungry for refuge.

Treasure

Do not be fooled
by shiny trinkets for sale
or pressured to purchase.

This is the story
of a kingdom's treasure
embodied, incarnate,
God so in love with the world
that heaven put on skin
and came to live with us.

Your shape is priceless
and your breath is costly.
Your presence is rich and
your embrace holds value.

Go, find fortune in one another.

LIGHT

There is perhaps
nothing older than the desire
to light a candle in the darkness,
to wait with the flicker
while shadows soak up everything
that is not the one thing.

There is perhaps
nothing more beautiful than waiting
in the dark for a word and a flame
to come and complicate
what has been hidden long enough,
to reimagine love right here.

PROMISE

Every time God makes
a covenant with creation—
the people and the nations,
the divine is leaning in.

Limitless power
declares limits for itself,
choosing a real connection
over and against everything else.

Heaven keeps coming near,
until one day, God is feeding
at the breast of one who whispers
sacred promises right back.

Fulfill

We have been keeping the law
like shallow breaths
too many too fast and never enough.

We have been keeping the peace,
covering, containing, concealing
a tension meant to transform.

We have been keeping the blessing
stopping its flow to cache and amass,
still it drips through fingers to get free.

Come into our keeping and show us
what it looks like to be filled and flooded,
made whole by things we thought were scarce.

Manger

They were more function than fashion
that first night in Bethlehem,
the trough cleared of scraps and slop
to make room for the One
who would nourish the whole creation
with good things, who would fast and fish,
feed multitudes and set bigger tables,
who would break bread and bless it and declare
his own flesh a feast that never ends.

Did the livestock and locals know
that love had come that first night in Bethlehem
when soggy leftovers were exchanged
for the full presence of God in their midst?

Census

It is one thing to be counted
like simple facts and figures
for the sake of a strategy
slim and distant, plans
that benefit a few already plush
with privilege and reserves.

And another to be counted,
included, and considered
part of a greater testimony,
a bigger picture that honors
to our humble portions and
the cracks in our becoming.

ABIDE

My son's first word was meno
though the other adults in his life
shrugged it off as a trying sound.

But I knew this was Greek,
one of John's favorite verbs
for the way God shows up to

dwell
live
stay
remain
come alongside
wait
set up camp
be present
abide.

I knew he was preaching
to my anxious and milky body:
be here. be right here.

Womb

From the beginning
God trusted her,
and God trusted her body
and God trusted her with her body.

In the beginning
it was dark and chaotic,
warm and beating with the rhythm
of breath and blood, life all around.

In the beginning
it was nothing and it was everything,
the strong and able frame
of one who said, Yes.

In the beginning
it was both safe and vulnerable,
a salvation story born of her body
and everything it already knew.

PONDER

The magi bring gifts
for woman and her child,
three sermons in one
and a warning besides.

Gold for a king,
whose reign lasts forever
across time and space,
a commonwealth for all.

Frankincense to burn,
a scent to rise
from altar to heaven,
declaring the divine is here.

Myrrh for burial, oil
to embalm the One,
whose death breaks death
and gives life the last word.

Their warning is timely
for these things have begun,
and while there is time to ponder,
it is also time to run.

GLORY

There is glory
in the way you
tell the truth with love
laugh from your belly
glow with gratitude
decline with autonomy
honor the silence
stand in the tension
dance and twirl in chaos
feel the weight with another
resist by being present
come home to yourself
crowned by the One
who claims you wild and free.

REPENT

Do not holler over your shoulder
or crane your neck to see
a portion of where you have been,
but rather turn your whole body around

and plant your feet anew.
Prepare for something whole,
healing and restoration that

summons your posture and attention.
Listen to the distance and longing,
squaring shoulders for repair

and careful motion in this direction.
Come home to yourself by way of
truth about whose you are, reclaimed
by a relentless mercy that waits.

PATH

The way we travel this world
has never been in straight lines.
These paths wind and wander
tangle and tarry so that
every tale is solitary without

becoming separate from the whole.
For paths we wish would ease,
and that God would find
the straightest route into our mess,
into our hearts and homes and lives,
to know and love our tangled ways,
what it is to be both bound and free.

MAGNIFY

When the world gets loud
with cheap banter and strobes
with interruptions that numb senses,

we can get very small.
Do not shovel the whole driveway

but find a single snowflake to worship.
Set aside the lists of gifts to buy,

and remember you are a gift to behold.
Get very small until the whole cosmos comes
into view and the only words you can find
are for praise and thanks and awe.

ANOINT

The oil cannot shine
without a surface, skin
that glows with good purpose
and the call to something

impossible on your own.
The oil cannot shine
until it finds a host
for fragrance and focus,
an aurora to frame God's invitation,
your help in doing a new thing.

STRETCH

We have been stretched,
made surprisingly limber
by a plague that both

bears down and unchains.
If you can feel yesterday
in the pull of your muscles,
you are not alone. It is desperate

to fold us into what was.
Keep stretching, Beloved.
Gasp and fill your lungs with
tender courage to keep
what has grown from shrinking.

HOPE

I was too young to remember
when they splashed
my forehead with tap water
and spoke promises over my life,

big mysteries pulled down for me.
Hope is like a glassy thread tied
one end to that day and the other
to my body, hidden in plain sight
so I cannot snip it with shears

and run off into the shadows alone.
Hope is like the reach of the thread,
its full length tangled but never taught,
infinite perhaps, a slack reminder that
there is much more to come and

I am worth finding every time.

Savior

There is One who comes
to save the whole world,
to overcome death,
righting what is wrong and

reclaiming every living thing.
There is One who comes
to save the whole world,

and that someone is not me.
When I remember that
I am not the savior of the world,
my calendar clears a bit and
I recognize more opportunities

for being redeemed with love.

DREAM

There is space in between
deep slumber and waking
when tender bodies and spirits

warm to heaven's whispers.
Here, in the hazy in-between,
we can recognize the rigid expectations

for the gentle guideposts intended.
Here, in the hours in between,
where midnight asks a little less,

we linger unguarded and free.
Here, in the space in between
this world and the next, we find
courage to push unholy limits and rise.

MESSENGER

Don't shoot the messenger,
the herald announcing a thing
that moves in and through them,
though is not theirs to keep or control,
a word that has a life of its own

and a telling that changes them too.
Don't shoot the messenger
because it will not stop a holy thing
from sneaking in and among those
it is meant to comfort and afflict,
it will not stop because you are angry

or determined to stay just the same.

COMFORT

'Tis the season for a song
that bursts from her lungs
about afflicting the comfortable

and casting the mighty down.
Not in vain nor to spite but
to reframe the detached ease
of some for the sake of all;
to carve out more open space
where assumptions reign,
where we sigh and submit.

This is how it always is.
'Tis the season for a song
that bursts from our lungs
about holy comfort that's coming

to satisfy the whole world.

Joy

There is a deep well in me,
and it draws from divine delight

for who I already am.
It fills and quenches so that
I overflow with satisfaction and

spring with signs of life.
When I gush, it is easy because
the goodness does not come from me

but rather through me.
When I laugh, I am opened
by the motion and moved
by heaven primrose and here.

Blessings for the Twelve Days of Christmas

For Christmas Day

Today is for marvel and praise,
celebrating the collision of love
and unbreakable connection with
the God who gets small and near
enough to know our mortality,
who makes dauntless promises
and find a way into every generation
with a Word and a breath that live!

FOR TWELVE WHOLE DAYS

✳ ✳ ✳ ✳ ✳ ✳ ✳ ✳ ✳ ✳ ✳

This love is brewed in slow trimesters,
taking time to be born even while
we spend the day at a reckless pace.
This love is a tide, one dozen days
pulling, a season stirring the earth

from moments to movements.
There is One who builds Life
in our hopes and fears,
who is revealed in our restlessness
so that we cannot box up or hide away
the sacred revolution heaven has planned—
it is already accomplished and on the way.

For Holiday Fatigue

This blessing knows how hard you tried
to make memories and keep covenants,

to conjure magic when no one was looking.
And it knows your fullness depends upon time
to recover in the wake of giving so much,

for in that rest, you will receive gift and grace.
So stop to see and know the world goes on
without you turning it, and in your stillness,
there is room for God's love to be born.

For Resisting the Metrics

✳ ✳ ✳ ✳ ✳ ✳ ✳ ✳ ✳ ✳ ✳

May your letting go
release what is already gone
and give you back
to God's delight

for your wild mortality.
This is a season for
resisting what is finished
and trying on measures
both ancient and new,
other ways of deciding

what's worthy and true.
Clumsy practice yields.
Your failing helps the whole.

FOR ANOTHER WAY

Empire says
Look no further than
these small choices and

the way it has always been.
Heaven says
There is another way
that tells the truth with love
and sets the whole world free.

For Loving the World

Remember, Beloved.
The call is not
to save the world
but to love it well
and behave generously
like all of it is worth saving.

For Packing It Up

When there are more
needles on the carpet

than on the tree,
it is time to pack it up
and put away the signs

of this sacred season.
Not the sacredness,
mind you. Just the signs

until next year.

For New Year's Eve

✳ ✳ ✳ ✳ ✳ ✳ ✳ ✳ ✳ ✳ ✳

Before resolutions, reflection.
Last year merits a moment
for setting free both grief and gratitude
for what has already been,

things within and beyond my control.
Remembering grants time to ask,
Am I running away from what was

or toward what still might be?
Perhaps this year's resolve is to
heal who I already am. My person
does not need fixing or replacing so much as

mending and gentle attention.
This requires deeper promises,
a sacred acceptance of the one
who deserves so much more than
this annual beatdown,

this withholding of grace and tenderness.
Begin by reacquainting yourself and
confessing the fear of being truly known.
That is resolution enough

today and every day.

For Slowing Back Down

Today knows you hustled
to manufacture magic
and meet expectations,
that your senses have been high
on the sugar rush of commercial cheer

and nostalgia chased.
Today knows you still believe
you must earn rest like paid leave,
that this festive hangover
is proof your striving has worked,
everything spent has produced

a faithful yield once again.
Today knows you need
the volume turned way down
so stillness can press on your speed,
and you sink into deep time
where the only thing that's true
gets loud and fills you with love.

BLESSINGS FLOW

God's blessing
is thoroughfare,
a movement rushing
that recognizes and rejoices
in God's goodness up close,
a story that pulls you in and keeps you,
even while it keeps expanding
to include everyone else.

FOR REENTRY

It is clumsy coming back
to the ordinary rhythms of everyday life
after weeks of music and magic
pumped into errands and tasks,
festival days that declared

something extraordinary for a while.
May your breath find a cadence
both old and new that recalls
the steady and standard routines
and delights in the details you save,
threading them through
one season and into the next.

FOR TWELFTH NIGHT

Build a fire
and stack it up higher
to light the whole night

with feast, song, and pyre.
Tonight is ablaze
with stardust inflamed
creation and cosmos
together reclaimed.

ACKNOWLEDGMENTS

I was skeptical when my editor Lisa Kloskin proposed this title. I told her I could probably come up with a dozen blessings for the Christmas Season, but not a whole book. She assured me that the team at Broadleaf was optimistic, and together we crafted a table of contents. Thank goodness for Lisa and all the people who shared titles inspired by their faith, longing, and lived experience.

I am grateful for the congregations I have served and the sacred ordinary seasons we have shared. Sierra, St. John's, Zion, and Bethlehem—thank you. Faith is communal and the wonder of incarnation comes alive in connection with each other. Those who prepare, pray, invite, welcome, decorate, sing, and tend to logistics behind the scenes help me believe in miracles.

For the writers, creatives, and compassionate colleagues in my life, and for the ways we challenge and celebrate one another. For introductions that become dear friendships and dream colleagues. You are radiant and remind me grace is not scarce.

For the extended family and friends with whom I celebrate Advent and Christmas, for all the hosts and guests who gather at tables, for all the ways we aim to be love for one another and the traditions that get flexible with time.

For those who labor and serve and give generously during this season, those separated from loved ones by distance or discord, those who long to be fully known or return home by another way. This book is for you and the One who has come to dwell and delight with you—your ordinary is extraordinary.